PLEASE REMEMBER
MY NAME . . . AT MY FUNERAL

and bring some Chocolate Chip
cookies with you

Fred Zobel

authorHOUSE®

AuthorHouse™
1663 Liberty Drive
Bloomington, IN 47403
www.authorhouse.com
Phone: 1-800-839-8640

First published by AuthorHouse   01/20/2012

ISBN: 978-1-4685-3488-7 (sc)
ISBN: 978-1-4685-3487-0 (hc)
ISBN: 978-1-4685-3486-3 (ebk)

Library of Congress Control Number: 2011963444

Printed in the United States of America

Any people depicted in stock imagery provided by Thinkstock are models, and such images are being used for illustrative purposes only.
Certain stock imagery © Thinkstock.

This book is printed on acid-free paper.

CONTENTS

Dedicated to

Mary and our daughters and their husbands,
Donna and Clarke Colombo
Debra and Kevin Agre
Deana and Gary Irvin
And our grandchildren,
Heath, Brittany, Chris, Clarke Jr., Mitchell, Nicholas, Dylan and Kyle

I can imagine a no more rewarding career,
and any man who may be asked in this century
what he did to make his life worthwhile,
I think can respond with a good deal
of pride and satisfaction:
I served in the United States Navy.
President John F. Kennedy
United States Naval Academy
August 1963

Foreword

My Dad died in 1970 after a year long battle with colon cancer. He was a very spiritual person, religious in service, and always involved in United Methodist churches. At his funeral on Christmas Eve, the ministers were eloquent and personal in their eulogies. I'll always remember several quotes from that service. One quote was, "Fred is now with his Christ at Christmas." Another statement made that day, "Fred was a gentle man and a Christian gentleman." Those words were so true—he was a humble and gentle man. I've grown to more deeply appreciate and treasure those words, and my father, through the years since his passing. A duet also blessed us at the service with a beautiful rendering of the Christmas song, "Oh Holy Night." I still approach Christmas Eve with joy, awe, celebration, and a touch of sadness that the dad who was a loving husband and father is not alive to talk to, hug, play golf with, and engage in other relational activities enjoyed by a father and son.

My mother died unexpectedly in December of 1995 of congestive heart failure. Her funeral was not as late in the month of December as my Dad's service. The minister who led her funeral service was also eloquent and personal. One of his quotes was, "Wini was always out front, leading the pack." So true! She was a woman ahead of her time in that, as a young woman, she badly wanted to drive a race car. Of course, that fantasy during her young adult era was not only frivolous, but also considered anti-feminine, if not downright anti-Christian. Who knows, in a later day she might have been a forerunner of Danica Patrick. Go Girl!

My sister, Jane, and I were blessed with a superb childhood. Both parents were committed to each other, and to our welfare. They loved us as deeply as two parents could and for that I'll always be grateful.

A continuing reflection about their funerals is that both services were personal without being sentimentally shallow. We celebrated their lives for sure but at the same time we were allowed to grieve their deaths during those services. I've always been thankful that the ministers pastorally led the services in such a way that we could do both—remember their lives with good memories and gratitude and feel a sadness that they were gone. I believe we were able to heal more evenly because of that pastoral act by those clergymen. That reflection is one of the driving motivators for the first part of this book since I've witnessed too often exactly the opposite.

My parents both liked to travel and experience adventures. Of course, there were certain limitations in their younger years as to how much they could travel because my sister and I were still in school, both parents were working, and finances limited how frequently we could travel. However, we always traveled somewhere once or twice a year even for short trips. After my Dad passed away, my mother was able to travel quite a bit since my sister and her husband, Vince, and my wife Mary and I were both Navy families stationed far and wide. Thus, there was always somewhere in the USA to do family visits on a holiday and other occasions. My mother even went as a passenger on a freighter ship.

In looking back at their love of travel I believe that Jane and I inherited those genes. Jane and Vince still travel around the country as they desire and Mary and I are full time RVers—we sold our house in Pensacola six years ago and have lived in our motorhome for six plus years. That love of travel and seeing the country is a primary motivating factor in the third part of the book. The second part of this book is a reflection of several experiences encountered through the years.

The phrase "bucket list" has become a common utterance in our society since the movie by the same name was produced several years ago. For those who haven't seen the film, I highly recommend it. The movie depicts two men who want to accomplish certain experiences on a list before they kick the bucket. Thus, the name "Bucket List."

One of the accomplishments on my "bucket list" is to write a book. The fact that the ten free copies that the publishing company provides will probably be the only ones printed makes absolutely no difference. If a critic decides to critique this book, well that's OK as well. Most importantly, I can check the box on my bucket list which says I finished a book. Make no mistake, however, everything written in these pages represents subjects about which I'm most passionate, bucket list or not.

The title of the book is explained in chapter one. I've always been fascinated about how we express and experience the loss of loved ones. Connected with that interest is how ministers deal with the subject, particularly in regards to their parish/synagogue members. Since I'm a retired United Methodist minister and Navy Chaplain, I've had to do both personal and professional introspection regarding the issue. Unfortunately, as previously stated, I've not always been impressed with the ministry, including my own, in the area of grief and meaningful funeral services. If nothing else, perhaps this book might stimulate a few clergypersons to reflect on their grief ministry.

As mentioned earlier in this foreword, I've also included several reflections regarding a few of my experiences through the years. Further, the book closes with a few episodes about experiences in and out of the ministry as experienced during our times as full time Recreation Vehicle (RV) travelers for the last six years. Lastly, of all the foods, particularly desserts, ever concocted in the kitchens of the world, nothing is better than a Chocolate Chip cookie—Nothing whatsoever!

Peace.

Fred Zobel

Husband, Father, Grandpa

Retired United Methodist Minister

And

United States Navy Chaplain

PART I

Chapter 1

"The 8 Minute Quickie"

I once knew a retired minister who was frequently asked to conduct funerals. He was in this role because he was a "contract" clergyman which meant that when the survivors or families of the deceased person didn't have a local church pastor for the service, the mortuary provided a clergyman to conduct the funeral service.

The particular retired minister that I mentioned would state that when conducting funeral services for persons unknown to him, he would take exactly eight minutes from opening scripture to the closing prayer. In fact, he said it in such a way that obviously he was bragging about the eight minute special, and thought it was a badge of honor. I would always irreverently mutter to myself that some family was about to receive an "eight minute quickie." In the process of that rumination, I was chagrined that the minister would think he was doing that family a favor with his grief ministry. Even more so because I knew this minister was a very caring person.

I actually sat through a few of his funeral services and witnessed the eight minute quickie. As advertised, the service consisted of a scripture, a brief Christian "Plan of Salvation," a closing prayer, and the benediction-all in eight minutes or less. If the family requested a song or two, the service was extended a few minutes but not by the minister. His goal was the "8 minute quickie." Nowhere in the service was the deceased person's name mentioned except in the format of the Plan of Salvation; if you want to see John Doe again, then you better follow the "Plan." For his grief ministry, remembering, celebrating, and mourning the life of a person took less time than getting the oil changed in a car or the tires rotated. Perhaps the minister's obsession with the eight minute special was both a reflection on his obvious priority of completing the service quickly, and our society's equal obsession with brevity in all things. In some manner, the minister may have only provided the pithiness that our society now seems to crave and demand.

In the end, how we provide grief ministry through the funeral/memorial homily and service is really an ethical issue and decision. By that I mean our actions (ethics) during those occasions of grief ministry and hardships indicate who we are as individuals and clergypersons. Aristotle seemed to believe that the manner in which we acted indicated the kind of people that we really were. Hopefully, as clergypersons, our pastoral service to members and strangers alike while they grieve indicate that we are people who act with diligence and compassionate hearts because that is who we are.

When considering a name for this book, I based the title on some of what I've experienced in my 45 years of ministry regarding the role of the minister during times of grief. I've witnessed personally, and experienced professionally, many fine, uplifting, and blessed funeral and memorial services. Conversely, I've too often been horrified at the opposite. This book is not a condemnation of personal clergy who engage in the practice of non-personal grief services. However, I do have some thoughts and a few questions as to how they provide for the care of surviving loved ones as practiced through the funeral or memorial service. That includes ethics, and the lack of pastoral concern sometimes exhibited by the ministers who seem unconcerned with the deceased person, or even their name as part of the service, except as part of a grand "Plan."

I think it's safe to say that we all hope our names will be mentioned at our funerals, even if the service is an eight minute quickie. Either way the service goes, quick or otherwise, please bring some Chocolate Chip cookies to munch on while visiting after the service.

Chapter 2

"Love—It's A Four Letter Word"

I remember working at a funeral home on more than one occasion when honoring the death of a loved one took second place to the need to enact the vitriol of family conflicts. Naïve is the person who believes that all family members are mature enough to put aside toxic relationships for a short time to honor a deceased family member. As any funeral home director or employee knows, the death of a loved one seems to exacerbate some familial conflicts rather than providing a sense of shared grief and healing. For some, a loved one's death is like pouring fuel on a hot fire instead of a unity of shared grace and healing for grieving souls.

For some families, love is really a four letter word—dirty, toxic, a reason to fight, and an engine that drives relational conflicts. Too bad, and oh so immature! However, family conflicts become so embedded in our emotional psyche, as any person knows who has taken Relationships 101, that they sometimes take a priority over many other issues and events. That includes honor accorded to a deceased family member.

If families who get into emotional, and even physical, fights at a viewing and/or funeral saw others committing that same action they would often be condemning and horrified. However, maintaining self-control to prevent them from engaging in that form of childish behavior is too often a forgotten art, thus the reason for the name of this chapter. Standing back from a conflict in which we have no emotional involvement is much easier. When there is, or has been, love and relationships involved in that conflict, our coolness and objectivity are often sacrificed to anger, hurt, egos, and foolish pride. I see these conflicts as an opportunity for the attending minister to bear witness to the Grace of God. All families have some form of brokenness. The clergyperson can often try to facilitate redemption even when the clergy involvement is neither direct nor substantial. In Hebrews, the tenth chapter, we're told by the writer to find ways to provoke one another in love and good deeds. What better clime than during the loss of a family member.

When family love is a four letter word and toxic relationship, particularly during the death of a family member, how wonderful the minister is who at least attempts to skillfully provoke those families in love with forgiveness, grace, and redemption.

The clergyperson whose minimal commitment to a sense of pastoral care, as exhibited with an 8 minute special, may find it difficult to provoke others in love and good deeds. That includes clergy who serve both as local pastors and contract clergypersons. Even a contract person can call a family member and discover a few important items and special events about the deceased person. However, that takes initiative and caring, and some contract clergypersons just aren't that willing to provide more time than is required by the contract, or the "Plan."

When I witness that ethical action, I'm all too reminded that ethics is really a set of choices based on our priorities. When the person doing a grief service has as his or her priority the quick completion of the service, as indicated when the deceased person's name isn't mentioned, my brain and heart seriously question the pastoral ethics of that worship leader. Although I'm the first to admit that my philosophy is harsh and judgmental, I have to wonder why it's so important to finish a service in less time than it takes to consume a breakfast. Next time that we plan a funeral or memorial service, please let us stop and reflect on our ethical philosophy as to how we provide a sense of healing and hope in the service to broken hearted people. May we always provoke one another in love and good deeds even in situations where love is a 4 Letter Word.

Chapter 3

"Being In A Room With A 600 Pound Gorilla . . . And The Exit Doors Are Locked"

This treatise took on a personal tone this week when I was diagnosed with Chronic Lymphocytic Leukemia, or CLL for short. Talk about a shot to the solar plexus-the unexpected announcement by the doctor that my routine blood tests indicated a problem with my blood platelets (too low) and white cell counts (too high) suddenly got my attention, particularly when she mentioned "blood cancer." I swear they must teach prospective doctors in medical schools to tell patients upon hearing potentially bad news that this isn't something right now to lose any sleep over nor worry about. Of course, my doctor told me just that, and she ordered another blood test in a few days to verify the first one. Oh, but don't worry, and don't lose any sleep over the first tests—said the doctor. Yeah right!

When I was suddenly faced with something as ominous as blood cancer that could be terminal, I felt an overwhelming sense of despair, helplessness and total aloneness. The Psalmist must have experienced that feeling when he wrote: "Why are you so far from helping me, from the words of my groaning . . . I cry by day, but you do not answer; and by night, but find no rest." (22:1-2).

To put the feeling in a down to earth, modern version—it's like being in a room with a 600 lb. Gorilla and the exit doors are locked. We live in a large motorhome but it felt tiny during the few nights until the second test. In spite of my doctor's good advice to not worry nor lose sleep over the "news," the motorhome felt like I was in a room with my emotional Gorilla and no escape. To make matters worse—it rained hard during those nights so I couldn't even walk around the RV Park. After that experience, I have a new appreciation for sleepless nights, and the overwhelming tension and futility associated with being pummeled in a room by a Gorilla with the doors tightly locked. Never have I wanted four days to pass so quickly so I could get the second blood test.

Well, the second test confirmed the first-the doctor was pretty certain that I had CLL. For any medical folks reading this, you know that CLL is a bad news/good news announcement. Yes, I have Leukemia, the bad news. However, if you're going to have Leukemia, CLL is the best kind to have. As several medical folks have told me, including my Hematologist, there is a good chance I'll die with the disease, not from it. Ok, but I would rather not have ANY bad news. But, since I have the "news," I'm thankful that I have the "good news" instead of only the bad.

Although I'm glad to get the "good news," I'm still wrestling with the Gorilla since its Leukemia nonetheless. And, I suspect, that will always continue although it now seems that, perhaps, there is an unlocked exit door. For that, I'm so grateful.

To the clergy caring for persons who have received the "bad news," let me mention a few observations. First, do tell the person that you'll pray for them and "gently" remind them that the Lord is always our Shepherd. Second, listen to the person without offering emotional pabulum, denial statements, and religious platitudes! Third, please do not talk of personal comparisons with the conditions of other persons. For the first few days while locked in the room with the Gorilla, I DID NOT want to hear any of the above, well-meaning attempts to help me feel better. When a person receives the "bad news," the sense of their own future mortality and demise takes over and leaves one uninterested and uncaring about the condition of other folks with ailments. Further, I wasn't interested in religious clichés, emotional therapy nor attempts to put me in a box of denial. At that point, I was far too internally oriented, maybe even selfish, to appreciate those ideas and well meaning attempts to assist. Clergy, and other readers, please resist the temptation to try and assist others with the above attempts to help a person deal with the "news." JUST LISTEN!

Unfortunately, listening to others is becoming a lost art except for those paid to be good listeners. I hope that someday we will re-discover this lost art. In my humble opinion, the best support a really good friend can offer is to be a good listener with the wisdom and patience to help another through a difficult period, and find hope at the end of the tunnel. Just LISTEN!

Thank goodness for my wonderful wife, Mary, who is one of the best listeners ever created by the good Lord. Although without a degree in listening techniques, she could easily and effectively teach a class to future and present clergy and others about the power of good listening as a therapy to help others when they're in a room with a 600 pound Gorilla and the exit doors are locked.

Chapter 4

"The Wonder of Support"

Former Yale Chaplain, William Sloane Coffin, lost a son via an automobile accident. After much soul searching, grief, and asking the eternal "why" question, Chaplain Coffin came to the conclusion that God gives us minimum protection but maximum support. What a powerful and poignant discovery by Chaplain Coffin.

I was recently reminded of his discovery as I listened to our good friend Janis Hand discuss the recent death of her husband, Don. Janis described Don's various afflictions and his demise from the ailments which eventually took his life. She did so with a voice and attitude of priority, faith and thanksgiving for their lives together.

Something that Janis said really impacted me while listening to her. She stated, and then emphasized several times, how much support she had received from friends, family, her church, and her faith. Janis spoke of how she had been touched by the outpouring of support. As she relayed her thanks for that support, I was again reminded of Chaplain Coffin's statement that God gives us minimum protection but maximum support.

Of course, much (perhaps most) of that maximum support comes from our sister and fellow humans on this earthly journey. To my ministerial colleagues, please help our church members remain alert to every opportunity to be part of the grief process that provides maximum support.

A parish or synagogue or other place of worship provides a magnificent ministry if it furnishes some form of support group for those in mourning, particularly if they've recently lost a spouse. The religious organization that does so must have an imaginative and persevering clergy and laity who will enact a grief ministry. When I write grief ministry, I mean one that isn't satisfied with a cookie cutter model that attempts to fit every grieving person into an identical syllabus. We all grieve differently—no surprise there. Women who grieve tend to be more inclined to sit and talk about their inner feelings of grief—not so with males. Maybe a male support group needs to meet in a gym, a golf course, a bowling alley, fishing trip, a book club—a male only support group. Most importantly, enacting a grief support group in which all persons are comfortable sharing their deepest loss, without pressure to grieve in a way that society deems correct, is a special gift from faith groups. It's so important to provide that place of safety in which persons can grieve without pressure to mourn in a way that society gives its special permission.

Chapter 5

"Doing Good Funerals"

One of the tremendous and blessed gifts during the pastorate of Dr. Henry Roberts at First United Methodist Church in Pensacola, Florida was his superb ability to provide meaningful and insightful funeral or memorial homilies. During my five years as an Associate Minister at First Church, I had the opportunity to listen to numerous sermons. Dr. Roberts had the reputation of "doing good funerals." The reputation was well deserved.

His homilies were good because he spent time thinking through the deceased person's life, their experiences, the circumstances surrounding their death, and the families who loved them. Never did I hear a funeral meditation by Dr. Roberts that wasn't well researched, and presented in such a way that grieving families and friends were helped in their celebration, renewal, and healing. And, that was partially driven by the fact that Henry knew his members.

From a pastoral viewpoint, it's my opinion that our church flocks remember and appreciate us mostly for our pastoral concerns and leadership. Yes, we're remembered and appreciated for good worship sermons, superb organizational acumen, community involvement (both ecclesiastical and secular), paying the bills, and missional emphasis. However, praying for our congregations, visiting them in the hospital and homes, being with them in both times of joy and sadness, and the myriad of other pastoral responsibilities all endear us to our members more than other clergy functions. And, that includes "doing good funerals."

Obviously, the funeral/memorial service sermon includes all elements of homiletical preparations. However, in my opinion, a pastoral commitment by the attending minister to his/her church folks will bring a greater richness and comfort in the family as the clergyperson leads a service that celebrates a life, mourns a loss, and brings hope to those left behind. "Doing good funerals" is one of the most significant and pastoral acts a clergy leader can accomplish.

A funeral led by a clergy friend while serving a United Methodist student pastorate in college years ago was for a person who committed suicide. I dare say that friend had little or no preparation for such a service even during seminary studies. I don't personally remember any preparation for doing funeral or memorial service homilies either in my initial training for a student pastorate nor in seminary. Yes, there were a few theological discussions about life in the hereafter—eschatology, to use a theologically technical term. However, nothing practical was provided that would bring any assistance to devastated families. And, certainly not any guidance provided for such a ravaging loss as the suicide of a loved one. If given the opportunity, I would make doing a funeral sermon a requirement in seminary, or even before if a clergy person is serving a student pastorate. It's the least we could do because "doing good funerals" is a basic pastoral act. Perhaps it's the most important ministerial gift that we can do in bringing God's healing Grace to wounded people.

Chapter 6

"A Wheel Came Off An 18 Wheeler"

Several years ago we were riding in our Recreational Vehicle (RV) as we approached Phoenix, Arizona on the interstate behind an 18 wheeler. Suddenly, a huge tire came off the back of the trailer. If you've ever driven a large motorhome, you're aware that at 60 MPH there is little room to maneuver without losing control when there is a sudden change ahead similar to a large truck losing a tire. It's even more poignant if you're also towing a car or trailer behind your RV.

Fortunately for us, the tire moved slightly to the side just enough that we were able to avoid hitting the obstacle. Had I hit that large tire, it would've certainly meant major damage to our motorhome or, even worse, a major accident. In a split second, I was able to get out of the way of a wayward 18 wheeler tire.

Sometimes we clergy need to "get out of the way" when it comes to grief being experienced by our flocks. By that I mean that it's important to just keep quiet when grieving folks are angry with

God, and express that anger. God DOES NOT need defending. We learn that in seminary. However, it's been my experience that many clergy forget that important lesson. Often that defense of God takes the form of pious or religious platitudes, logical reasoning about the loss, or some form of justification for the death of a loved one.

Please, fellow and sister clergy, when the wheel of grief hits people, get out of the way and let the experience happen without insisting upon inserting our theological brilliance.

Buddy Holly recorded a song in 1959 entitled, "Raining in My Heart." To quote a few lines: "the Sun is out, the Sky is blue, there's not a cloud to spoil the view, but it's raining, raining in my heart."

Grief is usually a flood in our emotional, mental, and spiritual lives. Even when we're smiling, it's often raining in our hearts. Grief can overwhelm us to the point that we feel as though we can't continue. Fortunately, there are many friends (including clergy) who help us regain our equilibrium.

Thanks to those clergy who don't let their egos become paramount, and are comfortable within themselves so that they are able to help their church members regain their emotional and spiritual balance when the wheel of grief hits them hard.

Chapter 7

"Hug A Funeral Director"

Our culture seems to avoid death at all costs. In 1963, Jessica Mitford wrote an eye opening, witty, and irreverent book entitled, The American Way of Death. The book elucidated a clear theory; the funeral industry had perpetrated a fraud on the American populace by charging exorbitant and often unnecessary expenses on the surviving families and making death appear to be a sentimental journey. Even the mysterious veil of the funeral home and embalming room was removed in the book. A classic book, for certain, on the entire issue of how we view death, and how we avoid it if at all possible. The book also made us look inward at our attitudes regarding death and our acceptance of it as part of the journey of life. In short, was the funeral industry only doing what we as a populace demanded?

Having worked in a funeral home for a short time, I've viewed the issue of death both as a clergyman, and as an employee who did whatever the boss told me to do. I must admit to a past degree of skepticism regarding funeral home employees in part due to being enamored with Jessica Mitford's book. Those employees and owners were often viewed in several prisms: ghoulish; money hungry; fraudulent; hard hearted; mentally unbalanced for being involved in the funeral business. Admittedly, my bias had little or no pedantic foundation.

Through the years, my opinion towards those in the funeral profession softened considerably. After working at the funeral home, I've become more endeared towards those who provide a necessary service. Yes, funeral homes, through lights, sounds, buildings, and accoutrements, do provide a soothing tranquility that softens the harsh reality of death. I suppose some folks view funeral home professionals with skepticism, maybe even cynicism. However, I've found those professionals as genuinely caring and concerned persons who want to provide assistance to grieving families that helps alleviate the pain and the trauma of death. Yes, there is a reason for those soft lights above the casket—it helps to soften the impact that our loved one is dead.

Next time you meet a funeral home employee or director, please be more appreciative. No, you don't need to hug them, just be thankful they are available to provide a service that is necessary and often misunderstood and underappreciated.

By the way, the funeral homes must make a profit in order to stay in business-that's the American way regardless of how much Jessica Mitford excoriated the funeral industry. However, those funeral homes do much to provide services to the poor or indigent in our society as well in order that they might bury their loved ones with some dignity. And, no, I'm getting no remuneration from a funeral home for the above statement. In fact, I can't imagine this book would be found near one of their "break rooms." However, after years of involvement both as clergy and employee, I have a much greater appreciation for their caring attitudes and services provided. OK—go ahead and hug a funeral director! And, bring them some Chocolate Chip cookies.

Chapter 8

"Osama bin Laden"

Today it was announced that Osama bin Laden had died during a raid on his compound in Pakistan. I'll not dwell on the politics of the "War On Terror" in this writing.

As a Navy Chaplain for thirty years, I'm so proud of our military persons who carried out the dangerous mission. Just as important was the action taken in regards to his body being removed and flown to a Navy ship and given a proper Muslim preparation and burial.

Although my human side delights that he is no longer a threat, my faith side is saddened that such evil exists so overwhelmingly that any response short of removing the threat seems flaccid.

I'm also proud of our Nation's decision to give Osama bin Laden a decent burial. I seriously doubt that the same courtesy would have been extended if the roles were reversed. I remember too well the horror of September 11, 2001 and the evil mastermind who planned it all.

I'm not jumping up and down with glee over bin Laden's death even though, as stated honestly, I'm thankful the threat is removed since I'm not an angel nor do I come close to being one. I wonder if the hoopla, starting with a gloating White House over bin Laden's demise, would've been better served with a low key acknowledgement that included a mixture of humility along with decreased celebration. Some of the same persons in politics who were energized the most over bin Laden's death were the identical folks who castigated George W. Bush's famous banner, "Mission Accomplished" a few years ago after the overthrow of Saddam Hussein in Iraq. Apparently, Mr. Bush wasn't aware of the banner's future appearance.

My point is that gloating political leaders would do well to keep their egos under control. Of course, those leaders are often served by staff aides who do their bosses harm by rubbing the noses of enemies into the dirt only to be slapped by those same adversaries at a later date.

Chapter 9

"A Great Day At Indy"

Along with 250,000 plus fans, we attended the Indy 500 race today with our daughter and son-in-law, Debra and Kevin Agre. The pre-race festivities were full of pageantry and patriotism. It's hard not to feel blessed at being an American during those occasions, and living in our wonderful country, warts and all.

The pageantry included the usual "Indy" specials including the singing of "America the Beautiful," "God Bless America," our National Anthem, Jim Nabors' "Back Home in Indiana," a military aircraft flyover, and the Invocation. All of the above presentations were meaningful, even spectacular, particularly the songs which we expected since "Indy" is the greatest racing event in the world.

Especially moving was the special tribute paid to the active military Soldiers, Sailors, Airmen, and Marines. As the car loads of military personnel were driven around the track, the thousands of fans rose to their feet and cheered and clapped. I was so proud of these military folks and happy that they received their well-deserved recognition. With a sense of probity, I also felt a tinge of regret because so many of us who served in Vietnam returned to the disdain of much of the country. It remains a sore point with me even today. Without being portentous, I believe that the men and women who served in Vietnam were never fully honored nor given their due.

After Vietnam, I retain a healthy skepticism towards many of the media, entertainment, political, educational, and religious "elites" who presently support military personnel. My skepticism, which occasionally borders on cynicism, but not bitterness, towards those self-appointed renowns is based on what I witnessed, during and after Vietnam, with the elites of that day, some of whom are still active in the same professional worlds. I remain skeptical towards the "elites." Their loyalty is too often thin, shallow, and based on what makes them look good, particularity within their own circle of like acquaintances and prejudicial opinions.

The most moving salute of the Indy pre-race presentations, and the most respectful, was when a bugler played Taps as part of the Memorial Day remembrance. To use an old cliché, you could've heard a pin drop amongst the 250,000 race fans during Taps. During that moving remembrance, I was reminded again how much Americans respect and remember their dead.

In case you have an interest in the words for Taps, the second verse is printed here.

"Day is done, gone the sun

From the lake, from the hill

From the sky.

All is well, safely rest

God is nigh!"

Years ago after retiring from the Navy, I was on contract with the Navy to do Protestant and non-denominational funerals or burials in the Pensacola, Florida area when families desired a military chaplain, retired or not. Of the numerous burials conducted, the playing of Taps by a bugler was the most moving and reverential part of the service. As Taps was played on those occasions, we were all reminded that, indeed, God was close at hand. I believe that was also true today at Indy; a reminder that loved ones were safely at rest with a God who surrounded them with His loving arms.

Chapter 10

"Celebrating A Life, And Mourning A Loss"

At the time of the death of a loved one, our culture places an inordinate emphasis on celebrating a life without mentioning that the passing also represents the requisite need to mourn that loss as part of healing. Too often, the phrase "celebrate their life" is used by friends, and family members, as a tidy methodology to avoid the fact that the deceased person is, well, quite dead.

We should celebrate the life of the deceased person unless they lived a horrific and vile life. Even then, the officiating clergyperson is called to provide a sense of dignity and respect towards the deceased, and any family or friends in attendance. With that said, we should celebrate a life. However, as mentioned in a previous chapter, we seem obsessed with avoiding death and the concomitant need to experience grief as part of the healing process. I believe our discomfort with accepting death as part of the human journey is often expressed in the statement, "celebrate a life," but without the attendant requirement to mourn the loss.

A number of years ago I watched on national television the "celebration of life" of a young, well-known movie personality who had tragically passed away. At the celebration, all of his friends jumped around in the ocean having fun, "celebrating", as they knew the deceased would want them to do. Now, how they knew that the deceased would want them to be frivolous after his demise is beyond my insight. More importantly, the grieving family members who were on a balcony overlooking the levity were doing everything they could to go along with the perceived requirement to celebrate the person's life, and not mourn his loss. However, their body language and saddened pauses between the celebration and giddiness of the young revelers betrayed their obvious sense of overwhelming loss. I do hope and pray that those family loved ones were able to mourn their loss, and to find healing from that loss even while celebrating that person's life.

In my opinion, wise is the clergyperson who is able to help family and friends to, yes, celebrate a life, but also deal with the mourning and sadness that is part of the grief and healing process.

Chapter 11

"Rest In Peace"

Yesterday, August 6, 2011, it was announced that a NATO force helicopter was shot down over Afghanistan with the loss of 30 American lives, including 22 Navy Seals, and several Afghan residents as well. I know there will be many tears shed and heartbreaks experienced by the families of those killed in that attack. I'm also reminded again of the sacrifices required of our military men and women, and their families. I personally do not believe that most other folks have any idea what it's like to be in a position where people are actually shooting deadly weapons at you. And, sometimes, whether you survive is not even in your own hands. That was certainly the case today for those aboard the helicopter.

Rest in Peace, God is Nigh!

I'm amazed that some of our government leaders wish to act as though we're only in some form of conflict with terrorists, not a war. My, my how words change world events—but not to the American and Afghanistan lives lost today.

Rest in Peace, God is Nigh!

I watched a morning TV show on a mainstream network which included a segment that was silly, shallow, celebrity obsequious by the TV host, all regarding some group of starlets who can only talk about the millions they're spending on themselves, and their future weddings. They certainly aren't part of our nation's economic problems. I suppose that group and the fawning TV hosts aren't too interested in Afghanistan, but 30 American families of men lost are real interested.

Rest in Peace, God is Nigh!

I saw a baseball game recently and some of the players acted as though the Star Spangled Banner was almost an insult, and certainly a waste of time. This disparaging attitude was disgusting by players who are talented with baseball gifts, and make millions because of those gifts even when their talents aren't that good. You could obviously see the disdain for our nation in their body language. Perhaps they should have to work like most people instead of living a coddled lifestyle. Yes, the national anthem means little or nothing to them, but respect for it means a lot to those Americans who lost their lives, and their families who now mourn the loss of their loved ones.

Rest in Peace, God is Nigh!

I love watching the July 4th celebrations from New York and Boston, and really appreciate the actor Gary Sinese hosting the New York event. Each time I move towards cynicism regarding so many of our citizens' apparent contempt for our nation, I'm renewed by the July 4th events especially when I hear the Boston Pops render "Stars and Stripes Forever." I hope the families of those Americans who died know how much the nation mourns with them.

Rest in Peace, God is Nigh!

For thirty years, I had the privilege of serving as a Navy Chaplain. During that time, I witnessed many occasions when heartbroken families experienced grief but with a sense of grateful appreciation for the nation served by their loved one. Whenever I see the Westborough Baptist Church protesters with their vicious and hate filled disaffections, I'm most appreciative of the men and women who serve, and who are willing to go into harm's way so that protestors of all persuasions and ideologies can have their say. The protesters who believe that America is an evil empire should thank those who serve, and their families. Without those servants, such as those who died, the protestors would begin to know what evil was really like, particularly if they shouted their protestations without the protective screen of freedom of speech

Rest in Peace, God is Nigh!

Chapter 12

"Oklahoma City-Bless the Children"

One July 4th weekend, Mary and I visited the memorial at Oklahoma City in America's heartland. The city is dynamic, full of life and activities and is the home of one of the most heinous and inhuman tragedies to ever strike one of our cities and its populous.

On April 19, 1995, the Alfred P. Murrah Federal building was bombed by a homegrown terrorist full of hatred, paranoia, and totally devoid of human decency. The tragedy claimed 168 lives including 19 children who were in a day care center in the building.

The building was almost destroyed by the massive bomb and is now gone, replaced by a breath taking memorial at the site of the tragedy. Next door, inside a building that was damaged by the blast but is now repaired, resides the Memorial Museum which Mary and I toured. Because of training that I had done with Navy Chaplains while on active duty in the area of Critical Incident Stress Debriefing, much of it from lessons learned after the bombing, I knew what to expect when entering the museum as visitors hear a recording of a routine Water Resources Board meeting that occurred nearby prior to the blast.

However, we weren't prepared for the emotional impact which occurred to us that day as we continued and completed the tour of the museum. Although emotionally and spiritually sad at such evil, we also departed with thoughts of hope, inspiration, and courage at how people can unite following a tragic event to bring some sense of peace and healing out of senseless hatred and chaos.

A consequential photo in the museum was a 3 word phrase painted on a wall that fateful day by one of the heroic rescue personnel—"Bless the Children." That phrase touched us deeply because we were reminded how fleeting life is, and continues to be. As was so overwhelmingly clear in the museum, many parents on that fateful April day in 1995 never dreamed that at 9:02 that morning their hearts would be broken and their lives permanently changed. Also, because of the many adults lost that day, numerous spouses, siblings, adult children, parents, and friends suddenly found themselves empty and full of regrets because time with loved ones had instantly vanished. Bless the children, indeed!

A few additional thoughts impacted us regarding our visit to Oklahoma City. First United Methodist Church is next door to the former building and was heavily damaged by the blast. Although the building was damaged, the church provided hope, as it should, by being a beacon of reassurance to everyone in the area for months after the bombing, even while healing from its own wounds. Other faith groups were equally supportive and mission minded, and remain so, including a stunning "Jesus Wept" memorial by the Roman Catholic Church adjacent to the memorial site.

I not only mention the above as an irrefutable statement of faith, but, also because the movement featuring Atheists and their apologists has gained a footing in the Internet and blogging world, and even with some mainstream media pundits. The notoriety the movement has gained is far more prominent, in my opinion, than its numbers justify. Such is our culture and the medium opportunities to propagate various ideologies, particularly in our New Age mindset. One of the focal points of the Atheist movement is its disdain for any religious importance or contribution. That obvious factoid isn't the start of a debate about that particular ideology. It is, however, an opposing viewpoint as to the good and healing power that faith groups bring to society, particularly during tragic occasions. Yes, religious organizations have many warts, weaknesses, hypocritical actions, and contemptible histories. However, more than other cultural organizations, the faith organizations represent healing and peace by bringing grace and forgiveness to broken people and broken communities. The beacons of atheistic organizations and governments of the last few decades are hard pressed to do the same—their legacy is one of darkness, doom, death and oppression. Certainly hope is not part of their ethos and policy.

A second highlight during the visit occurred the night we returned to the memorial site. Each of the 168 lives lost that day is represented at the site by a chair complete with the name of a victim who died. As darkness envelopes the area, each chair lights up. I simply cannot describe the spiritual and emotional impact that occurred when the chairs "lit up." It was like the lamps of Heaven turned on to remind us that while the Lord is not the author of evil, He is not helpless in the face of it. The message to us from the lights was that the Lord surrounds and upholds us with hope and peace and healing when we're overwhelmed by the darkness of evil, grief, and loss.

I also remembered that day and evening the many clergypersons who bring the blessings of hope and grace to both their flocks and the larger community during times of desolation and bereavement. How important the work of clergy is to bring words of comfort and hope since, as the crooner Willie Nelson sings so eloquently, it's "Funny How Time Slips Away."

Chapter 13

"Making Life And Death Decisions"

Years ago while serving as a Navy Chaplain with the Marines in Hawaii, the United Methodist Church provided a retreat for United Methodist chaplains stationed in our 50th state. Of course, some folks believed our duty in Hawaii was a "retreat" in and of itself. As someone commented, it was a dirty job but someone had to do it.

The speaker for our retreat was Bishop Dan Soloman, who was then serving as the Episcopal leader for United Methodists in the state of Oklahoma. His presentations were extraordinary in speaking to our spiritual and cultural challenges. One of his primary points was that in crunch moments in our lives, those momentous and crucial junctions, we act out of our hearts, not our heads.

I was reminded of this recently during a segment on a TV morning show regarding parents who spent $3,000.00 on a prom. A question arose about such an excess and was the cost over the top? The mother candidly admitted that, yes, it was over the top.

However, said the mother, it's the prom and it's my baby. In crunch moments, we act out of our hearts, not our heads.

Another example is the experience of funeral and burial expenses when a loved one dies. We want our loved ones cared for, even after their burial, as that represents our love and respect. Unfortunately, the decision as to what kind of casket to buy and other additional expenses is often made from the heart, not the head. And, that heart decision can remove us from a reasonable consideration as to financial resources. Therefore, some folks spend far too much on funeral and burial expenses. Our heads tell us what we can afford but our hearts guide us during those difficult times, and we're torn with tension and guilt.

A minister who has an effective pastoral relationship, even for a short time, might be able to gently assist a family during that difficult time when the heart can simply overwhelm the head when it comes to funeral expenses. Please note that I said "pastoral relationship." Certainly worship, educational, administrative, financial, missions, and community planning and accomplishments are vital and at times exhaustive for clergy persons. However, a pastoral relationship, in my humble opinion, takes priority over other functions particularly when a member experiences grief and trauma associated with the death of a loved one.

I'm a big fan of preplanning for funerals and burials. By making those important decisions before the death of a loved one, we act out of the head, not the heart, which gives us balance as to available financial resources and caring for a special person now deceased. A clergyperson can often provide a sense of self probity to members by gently leading them to a legitimate funeral planner before they have to make decisions that involve mainly their hearts.

PART II
Thoughts On A Few Subjects

Chapter 14

"Ignoring Bridges"

We've often heard that it's important to be careful about burning relational bridges with others since a person may need those relationships in the future. I've found that to be good advice, except when a person sticks a knife in my back. When that covert or overt act occurs, I usually lose any interest in maintaining a bridge.

During my ministerial career and retirement years, I've found a modern day infirmity that is worse than needlessly burning bridges. That malady is ignoring relational bridges. Ignoring bridges that bind us as humans include a careless refusal to return calls, the lack of basic courtesies in saying thank you, a sense of jadedness and cynicism towards persons who are good hearted, a lack of decency towards persons with whom we disagree, or an aura of hyper-arrogance on both ends of ideological spectrums.

A number of years ago, I took several hours to craft a message to an acquaintance of mine regarding a tour of a historic locale that deeply touched me. The tour had a related event that reminded me of something my acquaintance would quote often. Now, lest I sound whiny, I specifically stated to my acquaintance that the message could be handled any way the person desired so I didn't expect it to be shared or used.

However, I did, as a basic courtesy, expect a thank you since it was obvious that I put a lot of thought into the message. Upon not hearing anything, I even re-sent the email and then made a copy and left it at the person's office. Therefore, I'm absolutely certain the message was received. I never received even an acknowledgement of the message, let alone a word of "thanks for thinking of me." So, I wrote it off as another case of ignoring bridges that bind us, and left it at that.

Amazingly, I heard from the acquaintance in an email sent months later to a large number of people requesting money for a particular cause. While I had no trouble with that request, I found it incredulous that this person had no moral or relational pause about making the request. I wondered if others in the email "shotgun list" had also experienced a sense of ignoring bridges until the person wanted something from them.

I use this lengthy, and true, illustration to posit what I believe to be a malady that erodes our ability to improve human relationships; not burning bridges but ignoring bridges.

The results of that carelessness of ignoring relational bridges include: a lack of concern or interest unless there is a need by the careless person, a sense of hypocrisy when a need or desire does arise, an ignoring of basic courtesies. I wish leadership manuals, theological courses, and hospitality discourses would spend time on the ignominy of ignoring relational bridge

The emotional damage inflicted by ignoring bridges is particularly acute when a friend, church member, or family member needs a friendship during occasions of grief. The grief can include loss of a loved one, loss of a job, loss of a reputation, personal disappointment, or the debilitating weight of depression.

Today, please contact someone who needs a bridge—you will quite possibly touch them in a manner that is out of this world. Even better, take them some Chocolate Chip cookies. You'll be glad you did.

Chapter 15

"Really Being Somebody Other Than Just A Celebrity"

We're obsessed in our nation with celebrity worship. It seems the media has fostered an attitude that you're a nobody unless you've been on some reality show, The Today Show, Good Morning America, or hit it big in music, entertainment, sports, or politics.

A few days ago, I watched one of the network morning shows that has suddenly decided we need large doses of celebrity news as though we aren't already saturated with it. One such action taken was to create an instant "star" in music. When the young lady who became the instant celebrity was interviewed, she said she was so happy because she was now somebody.

At the risk of sounding like a pontifical, I wish to posit a different viewpoint of "being somebody."

"Being somebody" is a person who works to eradicate cancer or other diseases, sometimes in isolation, that will result in a healthy vicissitude.

"Being somebody" is a parent or parents who are doing everything they know how to teach their children good and healthy values, even if their children decide to ignore values and become troubled souls.

"Being somebody" is that volunteer who works to better their community without the glare of TV lights. Too many "celebrities," including some religious types, make their treks to help others only when the lights are on and some news type is gushing with words about the wonderful humanity of the celebrity. I believe those who only assist others in the spotlight are really poseurs.

"Being somebody" is the school teacher who labors daily to impart knowledge sometimes with little parental support, an insufferable bureaucracy, and not enough pay.

"Being somebody" is the cop who wrestles with the tensions of enforcing the law, keeping politicians happy and serving in the vanguard of keeping our society civil while remaining compassionate towards the populace, and their own loved ones.

"Being somebody" is the cleaning person who works hard to provide for a family or needs a second job to make ends meet or is doing manual labor to pay for school to better themselves.

"Being somebody" is a clergyperson who stays with a grieving family although they will receive little or no esteem for their pastoral service and care.

"Being somebody" is the person, clergy or laity, who provides help to hurting persons even when, like the Good Samaritan, they must make a personal, financial, professional, or spiritual detour to provide that assistance.

"Being somebody" is a politician who serves the public, and puts up with a media cynicism and sometimes public harshness that seems hell bent on making the servant some kind of debauched and pernicious monster.

"Being somebody" is a parent, or parents, who volunteer in their children's activities because being a good, loving, and dedicated parent is the greatest privilege in the whole world.

No offense to the young lady who can sing a tune and, in so doing, declared herself "somebody," a celebrity. Please! I'll take all of the non-celebrities in our communities who are committed to being good and productive citizens, parents, spouses and real people not inflated with their self-appointed importance.

Chapter 16

"An Expensive Dinner Date And A 50 Cent Bottle of Wine"

Even though I'm no longer involved in regular speaking engagements (mainly sermons) since retirement, I keep my membership in the Downtown Toastmasters Club of Pensacola, Florida. I continue that relationship because Toastmasters is such an excellent organization for its members to maintain speaking and communication skills along with challenging their mental percipience. Besides, who knows, after this book sells its ten copies I might be in demand as a public speaker.

One skill emphasized by Toastmasters is the need for voice projection. After all, what good is a speech if the audience cannot hear the speaker. Since I have a strong speaking voice, I've had to be careful about controlling my voice. A weak speaking brother I'm not.

While still employed at First United Methodist Church in Pensacola, Florida, I served voluntarily on a committee for one of the local financial institutions as part of community service outside of the church. It was an eye opening and wonderful experience including interaction with dedicated paid employees and other volunteer members.

Yearly, the institution held its annual members meeting, at least for the members in the Pensacola area. There were two dynamics at the annual meeting that I felt strongly about (and still do). I say the Pensacola area because all of the voting, including the Board of Directors election, was essentially decided by the few hundred in attendance although the worldwide membership numbers over 100,000 members. The efforts by several of us to include all members in the voting for the Board of Directors never got to first base, to use a sports metaphor, amongst the sitting board even though other institutions make voting availability for all of its members part of its governance. As the saying goes—win some, lose some. Perhaps a passion will develop amongst the members to change that methodology. Certainly, the technology is available to enact that possibility.

Another part of the annual assembly was the location—a superb place with plenty of room, good food and drink, excellent and speedy registration and voting, nice prizes, good conversation, and a cheap and terrible speaker system, particularly the podium microphone.

Based on my Toastmaster and speaker training, I was acutely aware that every element of a meeting is important. If one of those elements is ignored the meeting can lose some or all of its vitality. I won't be so dramatic as to say the meeting was a bust with the sorry speaker system but there were a number of persons who complained about it after the meeting concluded. Some of the meeting leaders were not trained in the area of public speaking and it was painfully obvious. However, that was not a requirement for employees or volunteers. So, to be fair, not all of the complaints had to do with the sound system. However, when audience members are saying they can't hear the speakers or are cupping their ears, the inference is obvious—they couldn't hear nor understand.

With the poor sound system (and a couple of speakers not trained in the area), it reminded me of a person who arranges a superb date only to be defeated by the lack of an important detail. Or, to use my own metaphor, the excellent location and the poor speaker system was like a person having an expensive dinner date, and then buying a 50 cent bottle of wine.

I mentioned this shortcoming to the then CEO and he agreed and promised to correct the deficiency. After retirement, I left the institution so I'm uncertain if that change was made. Of course, as a basic rehearsal prior to the meeting, I encourage all speakers to practice and include checking out the speaker system to ensure that the excellent and well planned meeting includes more than a 50 cent bottle of wine.

Even if the speaker's content is thin, or the speaker isn't skilled with the medium, or the speaker reads all of his/her comments, please ensure the audience can hear the speaker. Buy the expensive wine as it's the least the speaker and the organization can do for its constituents. And, please, always have an abundance of Chocolate Chip cookies.

PART III

Chapter 17

"The Nomadic Lifestyle"

My wife and I are full time Recreational Vehicle (RV) persons. We've been queried on numerous occasions about the full time RV lifestyle. For certain, it's a nomadic way of life. Persons who commit to being an RVer must be adventurous, love to travel, able to exist without a plethora of "stuff," and resist the fear of the lifestyle inherent in the "what if" questions. By that, I mean what if there is a personal or family illness, the RV breaks down or blows a tire, the price of gas by the greedy fuel industry continues into the stratosphere, the grandchildren miss their Grandma and Grandpa (they will), the children need a built-in and cheap babysitter (even full time), or numerous plans have to be changed due to unforeseen circumstances (and they will).

Along with the "what if" questions are the "how to" questions. How do we do our banking, get our mail, pay our bills, find an RV park that's not a dump, see a doctor or dentist, and stay in touch with family and friends? Those are all legitimate concerns and easily resolved, particularly with the advent of the electronic age. There are numerous publications that assist with the "how to" questions so I'll not elaborate here.

The RV industry is huge! Our main problem is to refrain from enslavement to the myriad of items for purchase, vendors trying to sell those items, and RV parks seeking your business. Further, hearing the regrets voiced by so many who wished they had hit the road before health issues and/or a lack of energy demolished their ability to even attempt to experience the nomadic lifestyle is, in our opinion, a sad commentary on what might have been.

We've given talks to several groups who are interested in the RV experience. The first item that I mention to a group is that the way of life is not for everyone. That is not a statement of judgment. Instead, it's an acknowledgement that we're all different which, in my opinion, is a joy, and challenge, of the human journey. What an absolutely BORING world it would be if we were all alike—a bunch of automatons going through the motions. However, if you have or ever had what I like to call the RV Fantasy, and don't at least explore the lifestyle with questions, I believe you could miss an opportunity for which you might regret at a later date.

A few caveats:

—If you're a "homebody" and believe a 50 mile trip to a casino constitutes a long trip, you might not be an RVer;

—If your ego needs massaging by adulation during employment until you're carried out horizontally, you might not be an RVer;

—If you and your spouse or partner have difficulty getting along with each other or don't have a spirit of symbiosis, you might not be an RVer;

—If the mere thought of being flexible with your plans makes you apoplectic, you might not be an RVer;

—If your sense of personal worth revolves around always being employed even after one or two retirements, except for financial necessity, you might not be an RVer;

—If you're content to live in a social cocoon and only see the same people and socialize in the identical locales, particularly when you're empty nesters, you might not be an RVer;

—If you're reticent about meeting new people and must exist in a clique (not the same as an introvert), you might not be an RVer;

—If you must have a lot of stuff, even items that you'll never again use nor your children will ever want, you might not be an RVer;

—If you must always adhere to a clock, you might not be an RVer;

—If you're absolutely certain that your family cannot exist without you down the street or even in the same area, you might not be an RVer (more on the family aspect in the next chapter).

As you can tell from my enthusiasm, the RV lifestyle is a magnanimous experience. If you have even a hint of desire regarding the RV lifestyle, please check it out and see if it might be a fit. Please, don't ever regret a lost opportunity, and then lament in later years the missed encounter to be a nomad. And, oh yes, munch on some Chocolate Chip cookies during your RV deliberations.

Chapter 18

"Being A Nomad—Don't Procrastinate"

Mary and I have been full time Recreational Vehicle (RVers) people for six years. We sold our home in Pensacola, Florida when I retired from the United Methodist Church in June 2005. We sold, gave to others, and/or donated most of our "stuff," including my professional books, and hit the road. We've not missed our stuff and, for certain, Mary hasn't missed doing the suburban yard work at all. Fortunately, we were able to start RVing since our home sold fairly quickly.

Although our nomadic lifestyle isn't for everybody, it works well for us. We've found that there are a number of folks who've retired and indicate they would like to explore the RV experience but will never because they can't or won't move beyond the willingness to leave their "stuff." Or, they won't be adventurous enough to leave town and their comfort zone and go more than a few miles from their families. I realize that aging parents, personal illnesses or family needs sometime become the operative priorities. However, we see many excuses to avoid the lifestyle wrapped up in the futility of procrastination. Some folks tell us they can't begin this lifestyle because their parents are senior citizens and they may get sick. Yes, that's true. But, their parents may also outlive them. Unless there's an active illness or debilitation, the use of aging parents can become a convenient excuse to refrain from doing that which some folks do not wish to do in the first place. And, that's quite OK as long as they're willing to be honest with themselves and admit their reluctance.

Also, we hear folks say they couldn't be RVers because they have to care for the grandkids. Or, they couldn't go more than a few days without seeing the grandchildren. Please! My reaction to this is "baloney." We love our grandchildren dearly but our children need to raise their own children. And, we love to see our grandchildren as frequently as possible. However, at this stage of our lives, we still wish to explore the country and experience new adventures. Plus, as the grandchildren get older, they want to do less with us anyway!

I recently had a conversation at a party with an energetic and spunky lady who showed much interest in our fulltime lifestyle. As she asked questions and we tried to provide answers, it was obvious from her statements that "they" planned to RV but never got the chance due to personal reasons. She made those statements with tears in her eyes and a deep sense of regret that the RV dream wasn't fulfilled. Obviously, she and her partner had procrastinated with their decision until it was too late. Oh, how we lament the regrets in our lives. If you're interested in the lifestyle, by all means do research, talk to RVers, and consider the pros and cons. Most importantly, if you're interested at all in the RV modus vivendi, please don't procrastinate and miss an opportunity for which you might regret.

If persons don't care for the RV lifestyle, either full time or part time, that is fine. But, I encourage people to refrain from using their families, or an obsession with stuff, as an excuse to miss the wonderful and fulfilling opportunity to be an RVer.

Chapter 19

"Buying And Keeping An RV"

RVers travel and live in various models. The motorhomes are divided into Class A which looks like a bus, Class B which is usually an extended van, or a Class C which is a vehicle that looks as though there is a bed over the cab. Trailers are either Travel Trailers which hook to the back of a van, car, or truck while 5th wheel trailers are vehicles that hook to the bed of a pickup truck. Most of us who have motorhomes, and are full time RVers, pull a car behind for transportation when we're stopping temporarily.

However a person decides to travel is usually determined by individual tastes, likes and dislikes, finances, and comfort levels. The RV industry is incredible in providing goods and services which adapt to the needs and requirements of RVers on the road or those who engage in short term camping or tailgating for sporting events.

If you travel by motorhome, you might hear it referred to as a coach. I've been asked the difference between a motorhome and a coach. My humorous answer is simply that it's a "snooty" issue—they're both the same. For some RVers, a coach sounds uppity and presumptuous whereas the term motorhome carries a tinny and riff raff reputation. Please! Since putting on airs is not one of my strengths, I refuse to call our motorhome anything other than that. Also, our Recreational Vehicle is not our coach or bus—it's our home which happens to be powered by a motor. There is also one brand of travel trailer whose owners sometimes give the impression that all other trailers are of an inferior class and quality. Names not mentioned here; the "snooty" might get offended!

There are many fine recreational vehicles on the road as well as some not so sterling. If you wish to explore buying a new or used RV, I encourage you to do research, talk to RVers who like the lifestyle as well as those who complain, and those who have decided it's not their cup of tea. Then, shop around at several dealers.

When looking, ensure you check the reputation of the dealer's service department. That is extremely important in the RV world since motorhomes and trailers are machines that have hundreds of parts which are vulnerable to breaking due to road conditions, fatigue, and possible mediocre quality. We've had five motorhomes and one travel trailer. We refuse to buy from any dealer other than one company in Pensacola, Florida. They are super folks, give us good deals, and, most importantly, have a first rate service department with quality service writers and technicians who take care of our "machine." Although I'll not mention the name of the dealer, you can call me and I'll pass it along to you. And, no, I'm receiving no remuneration from the dealer, just a promise that you'll be treated like family.

Chapter 20

"The Demise of Driver's Ed 101"

I'm uncertain when education officials decided that students no longer needed Driver's Education. Maybe it occurred about the same time as the completion of our nation's vast and connecting Interstate Highway system. Whenever it happened, those educators foisted on the American driving public a nightmare in which drivers simply do not know how to enter the interstate highways. Perhaps the educators who perpetrated that calamity were the same "smart" folks who convinced everyone that physical education was no longer important to the health, learning ability, and overall welfare of students. Of course, we all know that the lack of PE in schools is one of the reasons we now have an obesity epidemic with kids, and adults who use to be kids.

As an RVer, I'm here to tell you we have an epidemic of drivers ignorant about how to enter our interstate highways on the entrance ramps.

The scenario goes like this. A driver starts down (or up) the ramp to enter the interstate. Now, perhaps the driver is texting or applying makeup or checking ball scores on the I-Phone or still in shock over how much he or she just paid to fill the car with gas. Whatever the reason, the driver starts looking at merging with other traffic already on the highway about the same time he/she reaches the end of the on ramp. And, often it's only a cursory look in the rear view mirror. Of course, a driver that has more brains than a household gerbil knows you should be looking over your shoulder as soon as you enter the on ramp. When the entering vehicle carelessly continues, and the driver already on the highway (me) with a 43 foot motorhome and Jeep in tow suddenly needs the same space, it doesn't take an eighth grade dropout jock who believes Al Gore invented the Internet to know that something has to give. I can't stop on a dime nor move over quickly, if at all.

Now I suppose the drivers already on the interstate are supposed to think something like—"oh, there's Mr. Jones and we should just let him in even though his brain was left in a gutter somewhere when he got in his car—poor fellow!"

Perhaps Mr. Jones deserves our sympathy even as we're having a coronary trying to avoid him while his brain is in idle as he enters the highway. Of course, Mr. Jones may believe that the road is his and he has a right to it and other drivers need to get out of his way. That attitude is, unfortunately, akin to some of our rude populace which thinks only of itself and the heck with anyone else (ask a Flight Attendant for a story on the rudeness of self-centered clods).

Regardless of the reasons that people ignore a basic safety rule for entering a high speed and dangerous interstate highway, they're endangering all of us who are trying to avoid the nitwits who were deprived of Driver's Education 101.

On many occasions when driving the interstate highways, I know I've sounded to my wife like a person who talks to others via a telepathic medium. The conversation always occurs like this—"speed up, stop, look where you're going,"—and then laying on my air horns to wake the driver from their brain suspension, or scare the hell out of him or her (gender neutrality is necessary as there are as many females as males totally ignorant or careless about interstate driving).

Now, I can hear someone who believes it's their do gooder duty to be an apologist for highway morons. "Why not just move over a lane and let the person in?" I do when I can. However, when an 18 wheeler is on your side, you can't just move over. Besides, the entering drivers need to be looking and thinking ahead about their entrance, not counting on drivers already on the road to lose their teeth in the windshield to avoid their careless ways because they think they have a God given right to drive anyway they choose.

I believe the publishing house that I'm signed with only publishes ten free copies of this book. Except for family members who probably feel obligated to accept one of the ten, I'm under no illusion that this book will require more than the minimum. However, if nothing else, I hope this pontificating chapter will wake up someone, anyone, to the need to think ahead upon entering an interstate highway.

And, please, dear God, bring back Driver's Education.

Chapter 21

"Motorcycle Fantasies"

While meandering down the highway in our motorhome as full time RVers, I've seen multiple motorcycles on our highways. Every conceivable "bike" and "biker" has passed us—two wheelers, three wheelers pulling small trailers, Harleys, Hondas, BMWs, Kawasakis (suicide bikes with speed) old riders, young riders, skinny, overweight, with and without helmets (suicide again, with the breeze), single, tandem, loud and not so loud, male and female. I've found almost all motorcycle riders to be extremely courteous.

I have to admit that every time I see a motorcycle, I'm struck with a motorcycle fantasy (except for the suicide bikes). It just looks like so much fun. However, my fantasy is just as rapidly overcome with ominous fear. Some folks ask how in the world am I able to drive a big motorhome with Jeep in tow. My answer is always that once you get used to it, it's not bad at all—in fact, it's just so much fun. However, with a motorcycle, the fear is overwhelming. I equate the fear to the same phenomenon as going to the dentist and hearing that drill grind away at my bones.

There is one experience that I have with motorcycle riders that I don't understand to this day; why do some riders hug the middle yellow line on a two lane highway? I mean, come on, the rider is going to lose that argument if a puff of wind or blown tire throws the rider into my motorhome, or any other vehicle.

I once asked a female rider why some in the motorcycle family hugged the yellow line. I thought maybe it was a territorial thing—a mano a mano competition, a daredevil game, a desire to be seen by oncoming traffic (?), in a hurry to get to the morgue (death wish), arrogance. The rider to whom I directed the question provided a down to earth, common sense answer—no reason, said she, "kind of stupid, isn't it?" My response to that answer was a drop in the jaw, an incredulous stare of disbelief, a reminder of the comedian's edict, "you can't fix stupid."

Please, motorcycle riders, move over a few feet from that yellow line. If you come into my driving space, I may not be able to avoid you and the result for you will most certainly be deadly. Riding too close to that yellow line, regardless of the reason, may provide a bad hair day for both of us.

With that said the few of you who might read this and stop to gaze from the weighty tome you are reading now have the answer to the deep question—why do some motorcycle riders hug the yellow line? Stupidity, I suppose! Ah, but the fantasy goes on.

Finis "Preaching The Word One Season . . . . Cleaning Toilets
The Next"

Part of the RV world is the possibility to volunteer in governmental
campgrounds and/or work at private RV parks. The code phrase for
this experience is "work campers".

Work Campers may serve as camp hosts by checking in campers,
providing maintenance at campgrounds, cleaning restrooms, or
collecting fees. In private RV parks, the work camper becomes an
actual employee if provided monetary compensation. If there is no
money involved, the work camper is considered a volunteer and
usually provided a campsite as part of the agreement.

The activities can be varied, interesting, and even boring—like
any work experience. There are good "bosses," bad ones, some who
seem appreciative of the work campers, and some who see them
as tangible chattel. The nice thing about work camping is that if
a supervisor, boss or owner is less than ideal or even decent, or a
real dolt, all the camper has to do is crank up and depart the area.
Of course, like any regular employment, a work camper needs to
check out a potential job or volunteer situation in order to avoid
those conflicts if at all possible. After all, the primary purpose of
work camping should be to have fun. If the volunteer or paid work
position is drudgery for whatever reason, then it's time to move on.

The last two winters we have stayed in an RV park in Tucson,
Arizona which is close to our youngest daughter and her family. I
voluntarily led the worship services at the park for three months

during the winter season. It was a wonderful and challenging experience—bringing a message of hope and God's love to between 40-50 retirees and snowbirds each Sunday. I can't believe to this day how much I studied for the 15 to 20 minute sermons. Actually, that's the way sermonizing should be. Unfortunately, I know better because of the myriad of requirements of the modern pastor. Without trying to sound pedantic, the modern minister has my deepest sympathy in just trying to stay afloat. That's in addition to balancing needed time with their families.

After departing Arizona in May, we became voluntary camp hosts for the summer season at a county park in Pipe, Wisconsin on the eastern shore of Lake Winnebago just north of Fond du Lac. Again, it was a wonderful experience. We met a lot of super folks at the park and in the county office. My primary job was to deliver wood and ice, and clean the bathrooms. Mary did the administrative work and I did the outside stuff. When I say clean the bathrooms I mean every part including the toilets. Thus, the title of this final chapter, "Preaching The Word One Season . . . . Cleaning Toilets The Next."

The RV lifestyle fits us like hand and glove. It offers us the chance to travel without concern for a permanent domicile and weighty "stuff", the opportunity to see this amazing country, visit our geographically scattered children and grandchildren without being obtrusive nor intrusive, and be filled with excitement and wonder. We'll always have in our memories amazing anecdotes and experiential stories because regardless of how long this journey lasts, we live the RV lifestyle with anticipatory relish, and plan to continue doing so.

Whenever our earthly journey ends, we hope the minister will say, along with our names, those people knew how to enjoy adventure, and found this earthly journey one of excitement and down to earth fun, and Fred never ate a Chocolate Chip cookie that he disliked. And, now, another check off is added to my bucket list. Peace!

Acknowledgements

I've been blessed beyond what I deserve with a loyal, smart, patient, and loving wife, Mary. She has put up with me and is a true saint. She has gently pushed me to finish this book, and provided much of the manuscript corrections and rewrites that seemed endless.

Our only granddaughter, Brittany Agre, typed the original manuscript from my multitudinous and often confusing notes—yes, I wrote the manuscript the old fashioned way, with pen on paper. Besides being pretty and smart, Brittany, as the only female of our wonderful brood of grandchildren, is the apple of her grandpa's eye.

My thanks is also expressed to my English major son in law, Gary Irvin, who took valuable time in reading the manuscript and making editorial, grammatical, and punctuation suggestions and corrections.

I think back regarding the many persons who have impacted my life through the years. The list is endless, and with fear and trepidation I'll mention only a few. They, and many others, have made it possible to experience a joyous, fun filled, and enriching life that gives motivation to do something different, like write a book.

Ed Hardin was my childhood pastor and introduced me to this wonderful Christian journey. Charles Williams was responsible for "kicking my dragging rear" to get me moving towards the ministry—he also performed our wedding ceremony and is married to one special lady, Bettye.

Dear friends, both past and present, are appreciated because they have taught me the true meaning of friendship and positive relationships for many years. I mention them in that context because, at least for me, I would have a difficult time completing a book if my emotional status was always desolate and dejected. I love to laugh, and need to laugh, at myself and the sometimes craziness of our world. The dear friends of past and present have helped me laugh, and made sure that I never took myself too seriously.

I've been truly blessed with military Commanding Officers, chaplain and civilian ministerial supervisors, mentors, colleagues, Religious Program Specialists, musicians, secretaries and other support persons who have been a blessing. They're acknowledged in this space because they've been remarkable towards me, including those occasions when their advice and guidance stung a bit.

One chaplain who impacted me professionally is Larry Boyette. Larry was my chaplain boss in Pensacola and, after hearing me preach numerous times, told me over coffee one day the following:

"Fred, when I close my eyes and hear you preach, you sound like a harsh, angry, and almost mean person, and I know for certain that you aren't that way." For sure, his honest appraisal rocked me to the core, but, more importantly, forced me to do some soul searching and reflecting on my speaking style. Guess what? He was absolutely correct which launched me into a different style and attitude. Larry is a deep friend and I'll always appreciate his honesty, insights, and guidance. Thank you Larry!

Lastly, I especially appreciate the persons, in and out of my faith tradition, whom I have been privileged to serve during my clergy journey. Those who are served and ministered to must give their permission in order for that service to occur. Without their consent, service and ministry to them either doesn't exist, or is an abusive power by the servant bent on fulfilling an egotistical obsession.

One of my favorite singing groups is "Alabama." They recorded a meaningful song several years ago entitled, "The Fans." The song reminds them that as "the boys in the band," they can only entertain as a band as long as there are fans attending their concerts and buying their music. Implicit in the song is a message of thanksgiving for those fans because without them, they simply wouldn't exist as a musical group.

I look upon serving our flocks and larger communities in the same manner. Without their willingness to let us provide pastoral ministry, and put their trust in us to do good and, hopefully a minimum of harm, we as clergypersons would simply not be able to exist nor carry out our calling.

And, yes, many have brought me a plethora of Chocolate Chip cookies.

Notes

Chapter 4

Rev. Coffin's son died at the age of 24 in 1983. Coffin at the time was pastor of Riverside Church in New York City. He later wrote thank you notes to members of his congregation who helped to carry him through that devastating time: "you gave me what God gives all of us . . . . minimum protection and maximum support." He mentioned those words in his wonderfully moving sermon, "Eulogy for Alex," given ten days after his son's death.

Chapter 6

"Raining In My Heart"

The song was written by Boudleaux Bryant and Felice Bryant and published by House of Bryant Publications. Buddy Holly's life tragically ended in a plane crash in February 1959. He was 22 years old. The popular ballad, "American Pie," by Don McLean in 1971 was inspired by the tragic deaths in the crash of Holly, Ritchie Valens, and J.P. "The Big Bopper" Richardson.

Chapter 7

The American Way of Death by Jessica Mitford, was originally published in 1963 by Simon and Schuster. The book was revised in 1978.

Chapter 9

"Taps" is a musical piece played by the military to say it's time for lights out. The lyrics used in this writing are from the second verse. The term "Taps" originates from the Dutch term, "taptoe," and is used to conclude military funerals and burials throughout the USA. It is looked upon as the most touching and moving part of military funerals and burials. For a history of Taps, look at its beginning in 1862 by Union Army Brigadier General Daniel Butterfield. Taps was used by both Union and Confederate forces.

Chapter 12

"Funny How Time Slips Away" . . . . written by Willie Nelson and recorded in 1961 by Billy Walker.

www.ingramcontent.com/pod-product-compliance
Lightning Source LLC
Chambersburg PA
CBHW031240280526
45784CB00004B/1659